HOW I FEEL

MO T

DATE ....

BREAKFAST	LUNCH	DINNER
....		....
....		....
....		....
....		....
....		....

———— —— ——

SNACKS

....

....

....

....

TOTAL CALORIES

————————————————

PROTEIN CONTENT   FIBER CONTENT   WEIGHT   SLEEP   WATER   PROTEIN

———————— ——————   —————————— ....

OTHER

....

❤ **EXERCISE & ACTIVITY / MIND & SOUL**   SET / REPS / DISTANCE   **TIME**

.... | .... | ....

.... | .... | ....

.... | .... | ....

.... | .... | ....

.... | .... | ....

  6A 7 8 9 10 11 12P 13 14 15 16 17 18 19 20 21 22+

B=BREAKFAST   L=LUNCH   D=DINNER   S=SNACKS   E=EXERCISE   M=MIND

DAY (7)

MO TU WE TH FR SA SU

DATE ....

HOW I FEEL

BREAKFAST

....
....
....
....
....
_____   _____   _____

SNACKS

....
....
....
....

TOTAL CALORIES

_____

PROTEIN CONTENT   FIBER CONTENT

_____   _____

OTHER

....

LUNCH

....
....
....
....
....
....
....
....
....
....
....
....
_____   _____   _____   _____

DINNER

....
....
....
....

WEIGHT   SLEEP   WATER   PROTEIN

_____   _____   ....

 EXERCISE & ACTIVITY / MIND & SOUL

	SET / REPS / DISTANCE	TIME
....	....	....
....	....	....
....	....	....
....	....	....
....	....	....

6A 7 8 9 10 11 12P 13 14 15 16 17 18 19 20 21 22+

B=BREAKFAST L=LUNCH D=DINNER S=SNACKS E=EXERCISE M=MIND

HOW I FEEL

😃 😊 😐 ☹️
○ ○ ○ ○

MO TU WE TH FR SA SU

DATE ....

DAY ⑧

BREAKFAST   LUNCH   DINNER

....
....
....
....
....
_____ ___ ___   ....

SNACKS   ....
                              ....
....
....
....
....

TOTAL CALORIES

_____ ___ ___   WEIGHT   SLEEP   WATER   PROTEIN

PROTEIN CONTENT FIBER CONTENT

_____ ___ ___   ========   ....

OTHER

....

♡ EXERCISE & ACTIVITY / MIND & SOUL   SET / REPS / DISTANCE   TIME

....
....
....
....
....

 6A 7   8   9   10 11 12P 13 14 15 16 17 18 19 20 21 22+

B=BREAKFAST L=LUNCH D=DINNER S=SNACKS E=EXERCISE M=MIND

DAY (9)

MO TU WE TH FR SA SU

DATE ....

HOW I FEEL

BREAKFAST	LUNCH	DINNER
....		....
....		....
....		....
....		....
....		....

SNACKS

....

....

....

....

TOTAL CALORIES

_____ ____ ____

PROTEIN CONTENT   FIBER CONTENT   **WEIGHT**   **SLEEP**   **WATER**   **PROTEIN**

_____ ____ ____

OTHER

....

♡ EXERCISE & ACTIVITY / MIND & SOUL

EXERCISE & ACTIVITY / MIND & SOUL	SET / REPS / DISTANCE	TIME
....	....	....
....	....	....
....	....	....
....	....	....
....	....	....

🕐 6A 7 8 9 10 11 12P 13 14 15 16 17 18 19 20 21 22+

B=BREAKFAST   L=LUNCH   D=DINNER   S=SNACKS   E=EXERCISE   M=MIND

HOW I FEEL

MO TU WE TH FR SA SU

DATE ....

DAY (10)

BREAKFAST	LUNCH	DINNER
....	....	....
....	....	....
....	....	....
....	....	....
....	....	....

SNACKS
....
....
....
....

TOTAL CALORIES
_____

PROTEIN CONTENT   FIBER CONTENT

WEIGHT   **SLEEP**   **WATER**   **PROTEIN**

_____ _____ ....

OTHER
....

♥ **EXERCISE & ACTIVITY / MIND & SOUL**   SET / REPS / DISTANCE   **TIME**

....
....
....
....
....

🕐 6A 7 8 9 10 11 12P 13 14 15 16 17 18 19 20 21 22+

B=BREAKFAST   L=LUNCH   D=DINNER   S=SNACKS   E=EXERCISE   M=MIND

DAY (11)

MO TU WE TH FR SA SU

DATE ....

HOW I FEEL

BREAKFAST
....
....
....
....
....
_____

SNACKS
....
....
....
....
_____

LUNCH
....
....
....
....
....
....
....
....
....
_____

DINNER
....
....
....
....
....
_____

TOTAL CALORIES
_____

PROTEIN CONTENT   FIBER CONTENT
_____   _____

OTHER
....
....

WEIGHT   SLEEP   WATER   PROTEIN

======   ....

 EXERCISE & ACTIVITY / MIND & SOUL   SET / REPS / DISTANCE   TIME

....
....
....
....
....
_____   _____   _____

6A 7 8 9 10 11 12P 13 14 15 16 17 18 19 20 21 22+

B=BREAKFAST L=LUNCH D=DINNER S=SNACKS E=EXERCISE M=MIND

HOW I FEEL

MO TU WE TH FR SA SU

DATE ....

DAY (12)

BREAKFAST

....
....
....
....
....

_____ ____ ____

SNACKS

....
....
....
....

LUNCH

....
....
....
....
....
....
....
....
....
....
....
....

DINNER

....
....
....
....
....
....
....
....
....
....

TOTAL CALORIES

_____

PROTEIN CONTENT FIBER CONTENT

_____ ____ ____

OTHER

....

WEIGHT   SLEEP   WATER   PROTEIN

_____ ============ ....

EXERCISE & ACTIVITY / MIND & SOUL   SET / REPS / DISTANCE   TIME

....
....
....
....
....

_____ _____ _____

  6A 7 8 9 10 11 12P 13 14 15 16 17 18 19 20 21 22+

B=BREAKFAST   L=LUNCH   D=DINNER   S=SNACKS   E=EXERCISE   M=MIND

DAY (13)

MO TU WE TH FR SA SU

DATE ....

HOW I FEEL

○ ○ ○ ○

BREAKFAST

....
....
....
....
....
_____ _____ _____

SNACKS

....
....
....
....

LUNCH

....
....
....
....
....
....
....
....
....
....
....
....
_____ _____

DINNER

....
....
....
....
....
....
....
....
....
_____ _____

TOTAL CALORIES

_____

PROTEIN CONTENT   FIBER CONTENT

_____ _____

WEIGHT   **SLEEP**   **WATER**   **PROTEIN**

_____ _____   ....

OTHER

....

♡ **EXERCISE & ACTIVITY / MIND & SOUL**   SET / REPS / DISTANCE   TIME

....
....
....
....
....

🕐 6A 7 8 9 10 11 12P 13 14 15 16 17 18 19 20 21 22+

B=BREAKFAST L=LUNCH D=DINNER S=SNACKS E=EXERCISE M=MIND

HOW I FEEL

MO TU WE TH FR SA SU

DATE ....

DAY (14)

BREAKFAST   LUNCH   DINNER

....

....

....

....

....

_____ ____ ____

SNACKS

....

....

....

....

TOTAL CALORIES   WEIGHT   SLEEP   WATER   PROTEIN

_____ ____ ____

PROTEIN CONTENT FIBER CONTENT

_____ ____ ==== ....

OTHER

....

♡ **EXERCISE & ACTIVITY / MIND & SOUL**   SET / REPS / DISTANCE   TIME

....

....

....

....

....

  6A 7 8 9 10 11 12P 13 14 15 16 17 18 19 20 21 22+

B=BREAKFAST L=LUNCH D=DINNER S=SNACKS E=EXERCISE M=MIND

DAY (15)

MO TU WE TH FR SA SU

DATE ....

BREAKFAST

....
....
....
....
....

SNACKS

....
....
....
....

TOTAL CALORIES

PROTEIN CONTENT FIBER CONTENT

OTHER
....

LUNCH

....
....
....
....
....
....
....
....
....

DINNER

....
....
....
....
....
....
....
....
....

WEIGHT   **SLEEP**   **WATER**   **PROTEIN**

♥ **EXERCISE & ACTIVITY / MIND & SOUL**   SET / REPS / DISTANCE   TIME

....
....
....
....
....

🕐 6A 7 8 9 10 11 12P 13 14 15 16 17 18 19 20 21 22+

B=BREAKFAST L=LUNCH D=DINNER S=SNACKS E=EXERCISE M=MIND

HOW I FEEL

MO TU WE TH FR SA SU

DATE ....

DAY (16)

BREAKFAST	LUNCH	DINNER
....	....	....
....	....	....
....	....	....
....	....	....
....	....	....

SNACKS

....
....
....
....

TOTAL CALORIES

_____ ___ ___

PROTEIN CONTENT   FIBER CONTENT

_____ ___ ___

WEIGHT	SLEEP	WATER	PROTEIN

====== ====== ....

OTHER

....

♡ **EXERCISE & ACTIVITY / MIND & SOUL**   SET / REPS / DISTANCE   TIME

....
....
....
....
....

🕐 6A 7 8 9 10 11 12P 13 14 15 16 17 18 19 20 21 22+

B=BREAKFAST   L=LUNCH   D=DINNER   S=SNACKS   E=EXERCISE   M=MIND

DAY (17)

MO TU WE TH FR SA SU

DATE ....

○ ○ ○ ○

BREAKFAST

....
....
....
....
....

_____   ___   ___

SNACKS

....
....
....
....

LUNCH

....
....
....
....
....
....
....
....
....
....
....
....

DINNER

....
....
....
....
....
....
....
....

TOTAL CALORIES

_____

PROTEIN CONTENT   FIBER CONTENT

_____   _____   _____

WEIGHT   SLEEP   WATER   PROTEIN

OTHER

....

 EXERCISE & ACTIVITY / MIND & SOUL   SET / REPS / DISTANCE   TIME

EXERCISE & ACTIVITY / MIND & SOUL	SET / REPS / DISTANCE	TIME
....	....	....
....	....	....
....	....	....
....	....	....
....	....	....

6A 7 8 9 10 11 12P 13 14 15 16 17 18 19 20 21 22+

B=BREAKFAST L=LUNCH D=DINNER S=SNACKS E=EXERCISE M=MIND

HOW I FEEL

MO TU WE TH FR SA SU

DATE ....

DAY (18)

BREAKFAST	LUNCH	DINNER
....	....	....
....	....	....
....	....	....
....	....	....
....	....	....

SNACKS

....
....
....
....

TOTAL CALORIES

_____ ___ ___

PROTEIN CONTENT   FIBER CONTENT

WEIGHT   SLEEP   WATER   PROTEIN

_____ ___ ___   ══════════ ....

OTHER

....

♡ **EXERCISE & ACTIVITY / MIND & SOUL**   SET / REPS / DISTANCE   TIME

....	....	....
....	....	....
....	....	....
....	....	....
....	....	....

   6A 7 8 9 10 11 12P 13 14 15 16 17 18 19 20 21 22+

B=BREAKFAST   L=LUNCH   D=DINNER   S=SNACKS   E=EXERCISE   M=MIND

DAY (19)

DATE ....

MO TU WE TH FR SA SU

BREAKFAST

....
....
....
....
....

——————— —— ——

SNACKS

....
....
....
....

LUNCH

DINNER

TOTAL CALORIES

——————————————

PROTEIN CONTENT   FIBER CONTENT

—————— —— ——

OTHER

....

WEIGHT   SLEEP   WATER   PROTEIN

 EXERCISE & ACTIVITY / MIND & SOUL   SET / REPS / DISTANCE   TIME

....
....
....
....
....

6A 7 8 9 10 11 12P 13 14 15 16 17 18 19 20 21 22+

B=BREAKFAST L=LUNCH D=DINNER S=SNACKS E=EXERCISE M=MIND

HOW I FEEL

MO TU WE TH FR SA SU

DATE ....

DAY (20)

BREAKFAST	LUNCH	DINNER

....
....
....
....
....
_____ ____ ____

SNACKS

....
....
....
....

TOTAL CALORIES

_____ ____ ____

PROTEIN CONTENT FIBER CONTENT

WEIGHT

SLEEP

WATER

PROTEIN

_____ ____ ____ ========== ....

OTHER

....

♡ EXERCISE & ACTIVITY / MIND & SOUL | SET / REPS / DISTANCE | TIME

....
....
....
....
....

 6A 7 8 9 10 11 12P 13 14 15 16 17 18 19 20 21 22+

B=BREAKFAST L=LUNCH D=DINNER S=SNACKS E=EXERCISE M=MIND

DAY (21)

MO TU WE TH FR SA SU

DATE ....

HOW I FEEL

BREAKFAST

....
....
....
....
....

—————— ——— ———

SNACKS

....
....
....
....

TOTAL CALORIES

——————————————

PROTEIN CONTENT   FIBER CONTENT

—————— ——— ———

OTHER

....

LUNCH

....
....
....
....
....
....
....
....
....
....

———— ——— ———

WEIGHT

——————————
——————————

DINNER

....
....
....
....
....
....
....
....

———— ——— ———

SLEEP   **WATER**   **PROTEIN**

....

EXERCISE & ACTIVITY / MIND & SOUL   SET / REPS / DISTANCE   TIME

....
....
....
....
....

6A 7 8 9 10 11 12P 13 14 15 16 17 18 19 20 21 22+

B=BREAKFAST   L=LUNCH   D=DINNER   S=SNACKS   E=EXERCISE   M=MIND

HOW I FEEL

MO TU WE TH FR SA SU

DATE ....

DAY (22)

BREAKFAST

....
....
....
....
....

_____ ___ ___

SNACKS

....
....
....
....

LUNCH

....
....
....
....
....

....
....
....
....

DINNER

....
....
....
....
....

....
....
....
....

TOTAL CALORIES

_____

PROTEIN CONTENT   FIBER CONTENT

_____ ___ ___

WEIGHT	SLEEP	WATER	PROTEIN

OTHER

....

....

♡ **EXERCISE & ACTIVITY / MIND & SOUL**   SET / REPS / DISTANCE   TIME

....
....
....
....
....

6A 7   8   9   10 11 12P 13 14 15 16 17 18 19 20 21 22+

B=BREAKFAST   L=LUNCH   D=DINNER   S=SNACKS   E=EXERCISE   M=MIND

DAY (23)

MO TU WE TH FR SA SU

DATE ....

HOW I FEEL

○ ○ ○ ○

BREAKFAST	LUNCH	DINNER
....	....	....
....	....	....
....	....	....
....	....	....
....	....	....

SNACKS

....

....

....

....

TOTAL CALORIES

_____

PROTEIN CONTENT   FIBER CONTENT

____   ____

WEIGHT   SLEEP   WATER   PROTEIN

OTHER

....

♥ **EXERCISE & ACTIVITY / MIND & SOUL**   SET / REPS / DISTANCE   TIME

....	....	....
....	....	....
....	....	....
....	....	....
....	....	....

🕐   6A   7   8   9   10   11   12P   13   14   15   16   17   18   19   20   21   22+

B=BREAKFAST   L=LUNCH   D=DINNER   S=SNACKS   E=EXERCISE   M=MIND

HOW I FEEL

MO TU WE TH FR SA SU

DATE ....

DAY (24)

BREAKFAST

....
....
....
....
....

LUNCH

DINNER

SNACKS

....
....
....
....

TOTAL CALORIES

_____

PROTEIN CONTENT   FIBER CONTENT

_____   _____   ____

WEIGHT   **SLEEP**   **WATER**   **PROTEIN**

OTHER

....

EXERCISE & ACTIVITY / MIND & SOUL   SET / REPS / DISTANCE   TIME

....
....
....
....
....

 6A 7   8   9   10 11 12P 13 14 15 16 17 18 19 20 21 22+

B=BREAKFAST   L=LUNCH   D=DINNER   S=SNACKS   E=EXERCISE   M=MIND

DAY (25)

MO TU WE TH FR SA SU

DATE ....

○ ○ ○ ○

BREAKFAST

....
....
....
....
....

_____ ____ ____

SNACKS

....
....
....
....

_____ ____ ____

LUNCH

....
....
....
....
....
....
....
....
....
....
....

_____ ____ ____

DINNER

....
....
....
....
....

_____ ____ ____

TOTAL CALORIES

_____

PROTEIN CONTENT   FIBER CONTENT

_____ _____

OTHER

....

WEIGHT   **SLEEP**   **WATER**   **PROTEIN**

....

 EXERCISE & ACTIVITY / MIND & SOUL   SET / REPS / DISTANCE   TIME

....
....
....
....
....

_____   _____   _____

6A 7 8 9 10 11 12P 13 14 15 16 17 18 19 20 21 22+

B=BREAKFAST L=LUNCH D=DINNER S=SNACKS E=EXERCISE M=MIND

HOW I FEEL

MO TU WE TH FR SA SU

DATE ....

DAY (26)

BREAKFAST

....
....
....
....
....

SNACKS

....
....
....
....

LUNCH

....
....
....
....
....
....
....
....
....
....
....
....

DINNER

....
....
....
....
....
....
....
....
....
....
....
....

TOTAL CALORIES

_____ ____ ____

PROTEIN CONTENT   FIBER CONTENT

_____ ____ ____

WEIGHT   **SLEEP**   **WATER**   **PROTEIN**

OTHER

....

♡ **EXERCISE & ACTIVITY / MIND & SOUL**   **SET / REPS / DISTANCE**   **TIME**

....
....
....
....
....

 6A 7 8 9 10 11 12P 13 14 15 16 17 18 19 20 21 22+

B=BREAKFAST L=LUNCH D=DINNER S=SNACKS E=EXERCISE M=MIND

DAY (27)

MO TU WE TH FR SA SU

DATE ....

HOW I FEEL

BREAKFAST	LUNCH	DINNER
....	....	....
....	....	....
....	....	....
....	....	....
....	....	....

SNACKS

....
....
....
....

TOTAL CALORIES

_____

PROTEIN CONTENT   FIBER CONTENT   WEIGHT   SLEEP   WATER   PROTEIN

_____ _____   ==========   ....

OTHER

....

❤ EXERCISE & ACTIVITY / MIND & SOUL   SET / REPS / DISTANCE   TIME

....
....
....
....
....

🕐 6A   7   8   9   10   11   12P   13   14   15   16   17   18   19   20   21   22+
....

B=BREAKFAST   L=LUNCH   D=DINNER   S=SNACKS   E=EXERCISE   M=MIND

HOW I FEEL

😀 🙂 😐 🙁
○ ○ ○ ○

MO TU WE TH FR SA SU

DATE ....

DAY 28

BREAKFAST	LUNCH	DINNER
....	....	....
....	....	....
....	....	....
....	....	....
....	....	....

SNACKS

....

....

....

....

TOTAL CALORIES

_____ ___ ___

PROTEIN CONTENT FIBER CONTENT

WEIGHT   SLEEP   WATER   PROTEIN

_____ ___ ___   ====== ....

OTHER

....

❤ **EXERCISE & ACTIVITY / MIND & SOUL**   SET / REPS / DISTANCE   TIME

....	....	....
....	....	....
....	....	....
....	....	....
....	....	....

 6A 7 8 9 10 11 12P 13 14 15 16 17 18 19 20 21 22+

B=BREAKFAST   L=LUNCH   D=DINNER   S=SNACKS   E=EXERCISE   M=MIND

DAY (29)

MO TU WE TH FR SA SU

DATE ....

HOW I FEEL

BREAKFAST

....
....
....
....
....

SNACKS

....
....
....
....

TOTAL CALORIES

_____

PROTEIN CONTENT   FIBER CONTENT

____   ____

OTHER

....

LUNCH

....
....
....
....
....
....
....
....
....
....
....
....

DINNER

....
....
....
....
....
....
....
....
....

WEIGHT   **SLEEP**   **WATER**   **PROTEIN**

....

♥ **EXERCISE & ACTIVITY / MIND & SOUL**   SET / REPS / DISTANCE   TIME

....
....
....
....
....

🕐 6A 7 8 9 10 11 12P 13 14 15 16 17 18 19 20 21 22+

B=BREAKFAST   L=LUNCH   D=DINNER   S=SNACKS   E=EXERCISE   M=MIND

DAY 30

ARM ....

HIP ....

THIGH ....

CALF ....

.... CHEST

.... WAIST

.... BELLY

WEIGHT

BMI

....

NOTES

DAY (30)

MO TU WE TH FR SA SU

DATE ....

HOW I FEEL

BREAKFAST

....
....
....
....
....

SNACKS

....
....
....
....

TOTAL CALORIES

PROTEIN CONTENT FIBER CONTENT

OTHER

LUNCH

....
....
....
....
....
....
....
....
....
....
....
....

DINNER

....
....
....
....
....
....
....
....
....

WEIGHT   SLEEP   WATER   PROTEIN

♡ EXERCISE & ACTIVITY / MIND & SOUL   SET / REPS / DISTANCE   TIME

....
....
....
....
....

🕐 6A 7 8 9 10 11 12P 13 14 15 16 17 18 19 20 21 22+

B=BREAKFAST L=LUNCH D=DINNER S=SNACKS E=EXERCISE M=MIND

HOW I FEEL

MO TU WE TH FR SA SU

DATE ....

DAY (31)

BREAKFAST	LUNCH	DINNER
....	....	....
....	....	....
....	....	....
....	....	....
....	....	....

SNACKS

TOTAL CALORIES

_____

PROTEIN CONTENT   FIBER CONTENT   **WEIGHT**   **SLEEP**   **WATER**   **PROTEIN**

OTHER

....

♥ **EXERCISE & ACTIVITY / MIND & SOUL**   SET / REPS / DISTANCE   **TIME**

 6A 7 8 9 10 11 12P 13 14 15 16 17 18 19 20 21 22+

B=BREAKFAST L=LUNCH D=DINNER S=SNACKS E=EXERCISE M=MIND

DAY (32)

MO TU WE TH FR SA SU

DATE ....

BREAKFAST
....
....
....
....
....
_____ ____ ____

SNACKS
....
....
....
....

TOTAL CALORIES
_____

PROTEIN CONTENT FIBER CONTENT
_____ ____ ____

OTHER
....

LUNCH
....
....
....
....
....
....
....
....
....
....
_____ ____ ____

DINNER
....
....
....
....
....
....
....
....
....
....
_____ ____ ____

WEIGHT   SLEEP   WATER   PROTEIN

....

❤ EXERCISE & ACTIVITY / MIND & SOUL   SET / REPS / DISTANCE   TIME

.... | .... | ....
.... | .... | ....
.... | .... | ....
.... | .... | ....
.... | .... | ....
_____ | _____ | _____

🕐 6A 7 8 9 10 11 12P 13 14 15 16 17 18 19 20 21 22+

B=BREAKFAST L=LUNCH D=DINNER S=SNACKS E=EXERCISE M=MIND

HOW I FEEL

MO TU WE TH FR SA SU

DATE ....

DAY (33)

BREAKFAST

....
....
....
....
....

_____ ___ ___

SNACKS

....
....
....
....

LUNCH

....
....
....
....
....
....
....
....
....
....
....
....
....
....
....

___ ___ ___

DINNER

....
....
....
....
....
....
....
....
....
....
....
....
....

TOTAL CALORIES

_____

PROTEIN CONTENT FIBER CONTENT

_____ ___ ___

OTHER

....

WEIGHT

_____

SLEEP

....

WATER

....

PROTEIN

....

♥ **EXERCISE & ACTIVITY / MIND & SOUL**   SET / REPS / DISTANCE   **TIME**

....
....
....
....
....

🕐 6A 7 8 9 10 11 12P 13 14 15 16 17 18 19 20 21 22+

B=BREAKFAST   L=LUNCH   D=DINNER   S=SNACKS   E=EXERCISE   M=MIND

DAY (34)

DATE MO TU WE TH FR SA SU ....

HOW I FEEL

BREAKFAST	LUNCH	DINNER
....	....	....
....	....	....
....	....	....
....	....	....
....	....	....

SNACKS

....

....

....

....

TOTAL CALORIES

_____

PROTEIN CONTENT   FIBER CONTENT

____   ____   ____

WEIGHT   SLEEP   WATER   PROTEIN

OTHER

....

♥ EXERCISE & ACTIVITY / MIND & SOUL   SET / REPS / DISTANCE   TIME

....	....	....
....	....	....
....	....	....
....	....	....
....	....	....

🕐 6A 7 8 9 10 11 12P 13 14 15 16 17 18 19 20 21 22+

B=BREAKFAST   L=LUNCH   D=DINNER   S=SNACKS   E=EXERCISE   M=MIND

HOW I FEEL

MO TU WE TH FR SA SU

DATE ....

DAY (35)

BREAKFAST	LUNCH	DINNER
....		....
....		....
....		....
....		....
....		....

SNACKS

....

....

....

....

TOTAL CALORIES

_____ ____ ____

PROTEIN CONTENT   FIBER CONTENT

WEIGHT   SLEEP   WATER   PROTEIN

OTHER

....

♡ **EXERCISE & ACTIVITY / MIND & SOUL**   SET / REPS / DISTANCE   **TIME**

....

....

....

....

....

 6A 7 8 9 10 11 12P 13 14 15 16 17 18 19 20 21 22+

B=BREAKFAST L=LUNCH D=DINNER S=SNACKS E=EXERCISE M=MIND

DAY (36)

MO TU WE TH FR SA SU

DATE ....

BREAKFAST
....
....
....
....
....

_____ ____ ____

SNACKS
....
....
....
....

LUNCH
....
....
....
....
....
....
....
....
....
....
....
....
....

DINNER
....
....
....
....
....

TOTAL CALORIES
_____ ____ ____

PROTEIN CONTENT   FIBER CONTENT

_____ ____ ____

WEIGHT   SLEEP   WATER   PROTEIN

OTHER
....

....

....

❤ EXERCISE & ACTIVITY / MIND & SOUL   SET / REPS / DISTANCE   TIME

....
....
....
....
....

🕐 6A 7 8 9 10 11 12P 13 14 15 16 17 18 19 20 21 22+

B=BREAKFAST   L=LUNCH   D=DINNER   S=SNACKS   E=EXERCISE   M=MIND

HOW I FEEL

MO TU WE TH FR SA SU

DATE ....

DAY (37)

BREAKFAST

....
....
....
....
....

_____ ____ ____

SNACKS

....
....
....
....

LUNCH

....
....
....
....
....
....
....
....
....
....
....
....

DINNER

....
....
....
....
....
....
....
....
....
....
....
....

TOTAL CALORIES

_____

PROTEIN CONTENT FIBER CONTENT

_____ ____ ____

WEIGHT   **SLEEP**   **WATER**   **PROTEIN**

======= ======= ....

OTHER

....

♥ **EXERCISE & ACTIVITY / MIND & SOUL**   SET / REPS / DISTANCE   TIME

....
....
....
....
....

6A 7 8 9 10 11 12P 13 14 15 16 17 18 19 20 21 22+

B=BREAKFAST L=LUNCH D=DINNER S=SNACKS E=EXERCISE M=MIND

DAY (38)

DATE

HOW I FEEL

BREAKFAST

....
....
....
....
....

LUNCH

....
....
....
....
....
....
....
....
....
....

DINNER

....
....
....
....
....

SNACKS

....
....
....
....

TOTAL CALORIES

_____ ___ ___

PROTEIN CONTENT   FIBER CONTENT

_____ ___ ___

OTHER

....

WEIGHT	SLEEP	WATER	PROTEIN

EXERCISE & ACTIVITY / MIND & SOUL   SET / REPS / DISTANCE   TIME

....
....
....
....
....

6A 7 8 9 10 11 12P 13 14 15 16 17 18 19 20 21 22+

B=BREAKFAST   L=LUNCH   D=DINNER   S=SNACKS   E=EXERCISE   M=MIND

HOW I FEEL

MO TU WE TH FR SA SU

DATE ....

DAY (39)

BREAKFAST	LUNCH	DINNER
....	....	....
....	....	....
....	....	....
....	....	....
....	....	....

SNACKS

....
....
....
....

TOTAL CALORIES
_____

PROTEIN CONTENT   FIBER CONTENT

WEIGHT   **SLEEP**   **WATER**   **PROTEIN**

_____   _____   ....

OTHER

....

♡ EXERCISE & ACTIVITY / MIND & SOUL   SET / REPS / DISTANCE   TIME

....
....
....
....
....

6A 7 8 9 10 11 12P 13 14 15 16 17 18 19 20 21 22+

B=BREAKFAST   L=LUNCH   D=DINNER   S=SNACKS   E=EXERCISE   M=MIND

DAY (40)

DATE ....

HOW I FEEL

BREAKFAST
....
....
....
....
....

SNACKS
....
....
....
....

LUNCH
....
....
....
....
....
....
....
....
....
....
....
....

DINNER
....
....
....
....
....
....
....
....
....
....

TOTAL CALORIES
_____

PROTEIN CONTENT   FIBER CONTENT

WEIGHT   SLEEP   WATER   PROTEIN

OTHER
....

EXERCISE & ACTIVITY / MIND & SOUL   SET / REPS / DISTANCE   TIME
....
....
....
....
....

6A 7 8 9 10 11 12P 13 14 15 16 17 18 19 20 21 22+

B=BREAKFAST L=LUNCH D=DINNER S=SNACKS E=EXERCISE M=MIND

HOW I FEEL

MO TU WE TH FR SA SU

DATE ....

DAY (41)

BREAKFAST

....
....
....
....
....

SNACKS

....
....
....
....

LUNCH

....
....
....
....
....
....
....
....
....
....
....

DINNER

....
....
....
....
....
....
....
....
....
....
....

TOTAL CALORIES

_____

PROTEIN CONTENT   FIBER CONTENT

_____   _____

WEIGHT   SLEEP   WATER   PROTEIN

OTHER

....

♥ EXERCISE & ACTIVITY / MIND & SOUL   SET / REPS / DISTANCE   TIME

....
....
....
....
....

 6A 7 8 9 10 11 12P 13 14 15 16 17 18 19 20 21 22+

B=BREAKFAST   L=LUNCH   D=DINNER   S=SNACKS   E=EXERCISE   M=MIND

DAY (42)

MO TU WE TH FR SA SU

DATE ....

BREAKFAST

....
....
....
....
....

SNACKS

....
....
....
....

LUNCH

....
....
....
....
....
....
....
....
....
....
....

DINNER

....
....
....
....
....
....
....

TOTAL CALORIES

_____

PROTEIN CONTENT   FIBER CONTENT

WEIGHT   **SLEEP**   **WATER**   **PROTEIN**

OTHER

....

EXERCISE & ACTIVITY / MIND & SOUL

SET / REPS / DISTANCE   TIME

....
....
....
....
....

6A 7 8 9 10 11 12P 13 14 15 16 17 18 19 20 21 22+

B=BREAKFAST L=LUNCH D=DINNER S=SNACKS E=EXERCISE M=MIND

HOW I FEEL

MO TU WE TH FR SA SU

DATE ....

DAY 43

BREAKFAST

....
....
....
....
....

SNACKS

....
....
....
....

LUNCH

....
....
....
....
....
....
....
....
....
....
....
....

DINNER

....
....
....
....
....
....
....
....
....
....
....

TOTAL CALORIES

_____

PROTEIN CONTENT   FIBER CONTENT

_____   _____

OTHER

....

WEIGHT   SLEEP   WATER   PROTEIN

♡ **EXERCISE & ACTIVITY / MIND & SOUL**   SET / REPS / DISTANCE   TIME

....
....
....
....
....

🕐 6A 7 8 9 10 11 12P 13 14 15 16 17 18 19 20 21 22+

B=BREAKFAST L=LUNCH D=DINNER S=SNACKS E=EXERCISE M=MIND

DAY (44)

MO TU WE TH FR SA SU

DATE ....

○ ○ ○ ○

BREAKFAST   LUNCH   DINNER

....
....
....
....
....

SNACKS

....
....
....
....

TOTAL CALORIES

_____ _____ _____

PROTEIN CONTENT FIBER CONTENT   WEIGHT   SLEEP   WATER   PROTEIN

OTHER
....

♡ EXERCISE & ACTIVITY / MIND & SOUL   SET / REPS / DISTANCE   TIME

....
....
....
....
....

🕐 6A 7 8 9 10 11 12P 13 14 15 16 17 18 19 20 21 22+

B=BREAKFAST   L=LUNCH   D=DINNER   S=SNACKS   E=EXERCISE   M=MIND

HOW I FEEL

😃 😊 😐 😞
○ ○ ○ ○

MO TU WE TH FR SA SU

DATE ....

DAY (45)

BREAKFAST

....
....
....
....
....

SNACKS

....
....
....
....

LUNCH

....
....
....
....
....
....
....
....
....
....
....
....
....
....

DINNER

....
....
....
....
....
....
....
....
....
....
....
....
....

TOTAL CALORIES

_____

PROTEIN CONTENT FIBER CONTENT

_____ ___ ___

OTHER

....

WEIGHT   **SLEEP**   **WATER**   **PROTEIN**

❤ **EXERCISE & ACTIVITY / MIND & SOUL**   **SET / REPS / DISTANCE**   **TIME**

....
....
....
....
....

 6A 7 8 9 10 11 12P 13 14 15 16 17 18 19 20 21 22+

B=BREAKFAST L=LUNCH D=DINNER S=SNACKS E=EXERCISE M=MIND

DAY (46)

MO TU WE TH FR SA SU

DATE ....

HOW I FEEL

BREAKFAST
....
....
....
....
....
——————— —— ——

SNACKS
....
....
....
....

TOTAL CALORIES
————————————————
PROTEIN CONTENT FIBER CONTENT

LUNCH
....
....
....
....
....
....
....
....
....
....
....
....

DINNER
....
....
....
....
....
....
....
....
....
....

WEIGHT   SLEEP   WATER   PROTEIN

OTHER
———— —— ——   ============   ....
....

♥ EXERCISE & ACTIVITY / MIND & SOUL   SET / REPS / DISTANCE   TIME

....
....
....
....
....

🕐 6A 7 8 9 10 11 12P 13 14 15 16 17 18 19 20 21 22+
B=BREAKFAST L=LUNCH D=DINNER S=SNACKS E=EXERCISE M=MIND

HOW I FEEL

MO TU WE TH FR SA SU

DATE ....

DAY (47)

BREAKFAST

....
....
....
....
....

SNACKS

....
....
....
....

TOTAL CALORIES

_____ ____ ____

PROTEIN CONTENT FIBER CONTENT

_____ ____

OTHER

....

LUNCH

....
....
....
....
....
....
....
....
....
....
....

DINNER

....
....
....
....

WEIGHT   SLEEP   WATER   PROTEIN

 EXERCISE & ACTIVITY / MIND & SOUL   SET / REPS / DISTANCE   TIME

.... | .... | ....
.... | .... | ....
.... | .... | ....
.... | .... | ....
.... | .... | ....

6A 7 8 9 10 11 12P 13 14 15 16 17 18 19 20 21 22+

B=BREAKFAST L=LUNCH D=DINNER S=SNACKS E=EXERCISE M=MIND

DAY (48)

MO TU WE TH FR SA SU

DATE ....

HOW I FEEL

BREAKFAST	LUNCH	DINNER

SNACKS

TOTAL CALORIES

PROTEIN CONTENT   FIBER CONTENT

WEIGHT   SLEEP   WATER   PROTEIN

OTHER

♥ EXERCISE & ACTIVITY / MIND & SOUL   SET / REPS / DISTANCE   TIME

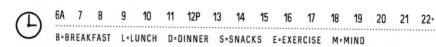

6A 7 8 9 10 11 12P 13 14 15 16 17 18 19 20 21 22+

B=BREAKFAST L=LUNCH D=DINNER S=SNACKS E=EXERCISE M=MIND

HOW I FEEL

MO TU WE TH FR SA SU

DATE ....

DAY (49)

BREAKFAST

....
....
....
....
....

_____ ___ ___

SNACKS

....
....
....
....

LUNCH

....
....
....
....
....
....
....
....
....
....
....
....

DINNER

....
....
....
....
....
....
....
....
....
....
....

TOTAL CALORIES

_____

PROTEIN CONTENT   FIBER CONTENT

_____   _____

WEIGHT   **SLEEP**   **WATER**   **PROTEIN**

_____ ====== ....

OTHER

....

♥ **EXERCISE & ACTIVITY / MIND & SOUL**   SET / REPS / DISTANCE   TIME

....
....
....
....
....

🕐 6A 7 8 9 10 11 12P 13 14 15 16 17 18 19 20 21 22+

B=BREAKFAST L=LUNCH D=DINNER S=SNACKS E=EXERCISE M=MIND

DAY (50)

MO TU WE TH FR SA SU

DATE ....

BREAKFAST

....
....
....
....
....
_____ _____ _____

SNACKS

....
....
....
....

LUNCH

....
....
....
....
....
....
....
....
....
....
....

DINNER

....
....
....
....
....
....
....
....
....
....
....

TOTAL CALORIES

_____ _____ _____

PROTEIN CONTENT **FIBER CONTENT**

_____ _____

OTHER

....

WEIGHT **SLEEP** **WATER** **PROTEIN**

....

 EXERCISE & ACTIVITY / MIND & SOUL   **SET / REPS / DISTANCE**   **TIME**

....
....
....
....
....

6A 7   8   9   10   11   12P   13   14   15   16   17   18   19   20   21   22+

B=BREAKFAST   L=LUNCH   D=DINNER   S=SNACKS   E=EXERCISE   M=MIND

HOW I FEEL

MO TU WE TH FR SA SU

DATE ....

DAY (51)

BREAKFAST

....
....
....
....
....

_____ ____ ____

SNACKS

....
....
....
....

LUNCH

....
....
....
....
....
....
....
....
....
....
....
....

DINNER

....
....
....
....
....
....
....
....
....
....
....
....

TOTAL CALORIES

_____ ____ ____

PROTEIN CONTENT FIBER CONTENT

_____ _____

OTHER

....

WEIGHT   **SLEEP**   **WATER**   **PROTEIN**

======== ======== ....

EXERCISE & ACTIVITY / MIND & SOUL   SET / REPS / DISTANCE   TIME

....
....
....
....
....

6A 7 8 9 10 11 12P 13 14 15 16 17 18 19 20 21 22+

B=BREAKFAST L=LUNCH D=DINNER S=SNACKS E=EXERCISE M=MIND

DAY (52)

HOW I FEEL

○　　○　　○　　○

BREAKFAST	LUNCH	DINNER
....	....	....
....	....	....
....	....	....
....	....	....
....	....	....
——— —— —	....	....

SNACKS

....
....
....
....

TOTAL CALORIES

————————————

PROTEIN CONTENT   FIBER CONTENT

———— —— ——

OTHER

....

WEIGHT   **SLEEP**   **WATER**   **PROTEIN**

EXERCISE & ACTIVITY / MIND & SOUL   SET / REPS / DISTANCE   **TIME**

.... | .... | ....
.... | .... | ....
.... | .... | ....
.... | .... | ....
.... | .... | ....

6A 7 8 9 10 11 12P 13 14 15 16 17 18 19 20 21 22+

B=BREAKFAST   L=LUNCH   D=DINNER   S=SNACKS   E=EXERCISE   M=MIND

HOW I FEEL

MO TU WE TH FR SA SU

DATE ....

DAY (53)

BREAKFAST
....
....
....
....
....

SNACKS
....
....
....
....

TOTAL CALORIES
_____

PROTEIN CONTENT   FIBER CONTENT
_____   _____

OTHER
....

LUNCH
....
....
....
....
....
....
....
....
....

DINNER
....
....
....
....
....
....
....
....
....

WEIGHT   SLEEP   WATER   PROTEIN

♡ EXERCISE & ACTIVITY / MIND & SOUL   SET / REPS / DISTANCE   TIME

....
....
....
....
....

 6A 7 8 9 10 11 12P 13 14 15 16 17 18 19 20 21 22+

B=BREAKFAST   L=LUNCH   D=DINNER   S=SNACKS   E=EXERCISE   M=MIND

DAY (54)

DATE MO TU WE TH FR SA SU
....

HOW I FEEL

BREAKFAST	LUNCH	DINNER
....	....	....
....	....	....
....	....	....
....	....	....
....	....	....
_____ __ __	....	....
SNACKS	....	....
....	....	....
....	....	....
....	....	....
....	....	....
_____ __ __	____ __ __	__ __ __

TOTAL CALORIES

_____

PROTEIN CONTENT FIBER CONTENT

_____ _____ ========= ....

WEIGHT SLEEP WATER PROTEIN

OTHER

....

♥ EXERCISE & ACTIVITY / MIND & SOUL   SET / REPS / DISTANCE   TIME

....	....	....
....	....	....
....	....	....
....	....	....
....	....	....

🕐 6A 7 8 9 10 11 12P 13 14 15 16 17 18 19 20 21 22+
....

B=BREAKFAST L=LUNCH D=DINNER S=SNACKS E=EXERCISE M=MIND

HOW I FEEL

MO TU WE TH FR SA SU

DATE ....

DAY (55)

BREAKFAST

....
....
....
....
....
_____ ____ ____

SNACKS

....
....
....
....
_____ ____ ____

LUNCH

....
....
....
....
....
....
....
....
....
....
....
....
....
....

DINNER

....
....
....
....
....
....

TOTAL CALORIES

_____

PROTEIN CONTENT FIBER CONTENT

_____ _____

WEIGHT

SLEEP

WATER

PROTEIN

_____ _____ ....

OTHER

....

❤ EXERCISE & ACTIVITY / MIND & SOUL

EXERCISE & ACTIVITY / MIND & SOUL	SET / REPS / DISTANCE	TIME
....	....	....
....	....	....
....	....	....
....	....	....
....	....	....

 6A 7 8 9 10 11 12P 13 14 15 16 17 18 19 20 21 22+

B=BREAKFAST L=LUNCH D=DINNER S=SNACKS E=EXERCISE M=MIND

DAY (56)

HOW I FEEL

○ ○ ○ ○

BREAKFAST	LUNCH	DINNER
....	....	....
....	....	....
....	....	....
....	....	....
....	....	....

——— —— ——

SNACKS

....	....	....
....	....	....
....	....	....
....	....	....

——— —— ——

TOTAL CALORIES

——————————

PROTEIN CONTENT   FIBER CONTENT   WEIGHT   SLEEP   WATER   PROTEIN

———— ——— ———   =========   ....

OTHER

....

♥ EXERCISE & ACTIVITY / MIND & SOUL   SET / REPS / DISTANCE   TIME

....	....	....
....	....	....
....	....	....
....	....	....
....	....	....

🕐 6A 7 8 9 10 11 12P 13 14 15 16 17 18 19 20 21 22+

B=BREAKFAST   L=LUNCH   D=DINNER   S=SNACKS   E=EXERCISE   M=MIND

HOW I FEEL

😃 🙂 😐 🙁
○ ○ ○ ○

MO TU WE TH FR SA SU

DATE ....

DAY (57)

BREAKFAST	LUNCH	DINNER

BREAKFAST
....
....
....
....
....
_____ ____ ____

SNACKS
....
....
....
....

LUNCH
....
....
....
....
....
....
....
....
....
....
....
_____ ____ ____

DINNER
....
....
....
....
_____ ____ ____

TOTAL CALORIES

_____

PROTEIN CONTENT   FIBER CONTENT

_____ ____ ____

OTHER
....

WEIGHT   SLEEP   WATER   PROTEIN

❤ EXERCISE & ACTIVITY / MIND & SOUL   SET / REPS / DISTANCE   TIME

....
....
....
....
....

 6A 7 8 9 10 11 12P 13 14 15 16 17 18 19 20 21 22+

B=BREAKFAST L=LUNCH D=DINNER S=SNACKS E=EXERCISE M=MIND

DAY (58)

MO TU WE TH FR SA SU

DATE ....

HOW I FEEL

BREAKFAST	LUNCH	DINNER
....	....	....
....	....	....
....	....	....
....	....	....
....	....	....

SNACKS

....
....
....
....

TOTAL CALORIES

_____ ____ ____

PROTEIN CONTENT   FIBER CONTENT

_____ ____ ____

WEIGHT   SLEEP   WATER   PROTEIN

OTHER

....

 EXERCISE & ACTIVITY / MIND & SOUL   SET / REPS / DISTANCE   TIME

EXERCISE & ACTIVITY / MIND & SOUL	SET / REPS / DISTANCE	TIME
....	....	....
....	....	....
....	....	....
....	....	....
....	....	....

6A 7 8 9 10 11 12P 13 14 15 16 17 18 19 20 21 22+

B=BREAKFAST   L=LUNCH   D=DINNER   S=SNACKS   E=EXERCISE   M=MIND

HOW I FEEL

😀 🙂 😐 😞
○ ○ ○ ○

MO TU WE TH FR SA SU

DATE ....

DAY 59

BREAKFAST | LUNCH | DINNER

....

....

....

....

....

—————— —— ——

SNACKS

....

....

....

....

—————— —— ——

TOTAL CALORIES

——————————

PROTEIN CONTENT FIBER CONTENT

WEIGHT   SLEEP   WATER   PROTEIN

—————— —— ——

OTHER

....

♡ EXERCISE & ACTIVITY / MIND & SOUL   SET / REPS / DISTANCE   TIME

....

....

....

....

....

 6A 7 8 9 10 11 12P 13 14 15 16 17 18 19 20 21 22+

B=BREAKFAST L=LUNCH D=DINNER S=SNACKS E=EXERCISE M=MIND

DAY 60

ARM ....

CHEST ....

WAIST ....

BELLY ....

HIP ....

THIGH ....

CALF ....

WEIGHT

....

BMI

....

NOTES ....

....

....

....

....

HOW I FEEL

MO TU WE TH FR SA SU

DATE ....

DAY 60

BREAKFAST

....
....
....
....
....

SNACKS

....
....
....
....

LUNCH

....
....
....
....
....
....
....
....
....
....

DINNER

....
....
....
....
....
....
....
....
....

TOTAL CALORIES

_____

PROTEIN CONTENT FIBER CONTENT

WEIGHT   SLEEP   WATER   PROTEIN

OTHER

....

EXERCISE & ACTIVITY / MIND & SOUL   SET / REPS / DISTANCE   TIME

....
....
....
....
....

 6A 7 8 9 10 11 12P 13 14 15 16 17 18 19 20 21 22+

B=BREAKFAST L=LUNCH D=DINNER S=SNACKS E=EXERCISE M=MIND

DAY (61)

MO TU WE TH FR SA SU

DATE ....

HOW I FEEL

☺ ☺ ☺ ☹
○ ○ ○ ○

BREAKFAST

LUNCH

DINNER

....
....
....
....
....

———— —— ——

SNACKS

....
....
....
....

TOTAL CALORIES

———— —— ——

PROTEIN CONTENT FIBER CONTENT

———— —— ——

OTHER

....

WEIGHT

SLEEP

WATER

PROTEIN

❤ EXERCISE & ACTIVITY / MIND & SOUL

SET / REPS / DISTANCE

TIME

....
....
....
....
....

🕐 6A 7 8 9 10 11 12P 13 14 15 16 17 18 19 20 21 22+

B=BREAKFAST L=LUNCH D=DINNER S=SNACKS E=EXERCISE M=MIND

HOW I FEEL

MO TU WE TH FR SA SU

DATE ....

DAY (62)

BREAKFAST

LUNCH

DINNER

....

....

....

....

....

SNACKS

....

....

....

....

TOTAL CALORIES

_____ __ __

PROTEIN CONTENT FIBER CONTENT

WEIGHT

SLEEP

WATER

PROTEIN

OTHER

....

♥ EXERCISE & ACTIVITY / MIND & SOUL   SET / REPS / DISTANCE   TIME

 6A 7 8 9 10 11 12P 13 14 15 16 17 18 19 20 21 22+

B=BREAKFAST L=LUNCH D=DINNER S=SNACKS E=EXERCISE M=MIND

DAY (63)

MO TU WE TH FR SA SU

DATE ....

BREAKFAST	LUNCH	DINNER
....	....	....
....	....	....
....	....	....
....	....	....
....	....	....
———— — —	....	....

SNACKS

....
....
....
....

———— — —

TOTAL CALORIES

——————————

PROTEIN CONTENT FIBER CONTENT

———— — —

WEIGHT   SLEEP   WATER   PROTEIN

OTHER

....

❤ **EXERCISE & ACTIVITY / MIND & SOUL**   SET / REPS / DISTANCE   TIME

.... | .... | ....
.... | .... | ....
.... | .... | ....
.... | .... | ....
.... | .... | ....

————————   ————   ————

🕐 6A 7 8 9 10 11 12P 13 14 15 16 17 18 19 20 21 22+

B=BREAKFAST L=LUNCH D=DINNER S=SNACKS E=EXERCISE M=MIND

HOW I FEEL

😃 ○ 🙂 ○ 😐 ○ 🙁 ○

MO TU WE TH FR SA SU

DATE ....

DAY 64

BREAKFAST

....
....
....
....
....

LUNCH

....
....
....
....
....
....
....
....
....
....

DINNER

....
....
....
....
....

SNACKS

....
....
....
....

TOTAL CALORIES

_____ ____ ____

PROTEIN CONTENT   FIBER CONTENT

_____   _____

WEIGHT

SLEEP

WATER

PROTEIN

OTHER

....

♥ **EXERCISE & ACTIVITY / MIND & SOUL**   SET / REPS / DISTANCE   TIME

....
....
....
....
....

6A 7 8 9 10 11 12P 13 14 15 16 17 18 19 20 21 22+

B=BREAKFAST   L=LUNCH   D=DINNER   S=SNACKS   E=EXERCISE   M=MIND

DAY (65)

DATE ....

MO TU WE TH FR SA SU

HOW I FEEL

BREAKFAST

....
....
....
....
....
_____   _____   _____

SNACKS

....
....
....
....

TOTAL CALORIES

_____
PROTEIN CONTENT   FIBER CONTENT

_____   _____

OTHER

....

LUNCH

....
....
....
....
....
....
....
....
....
....
....
_____   _____   _____

DINNER

....
....
....
....
....
....
....
....
....
....
_____   _____

WEIGHT

SLEEP

WATER

PROTEIN

....

♥ EXERCISE & ACTIVITY / MIND & SOUL   SET / REPS / DISTANCE   TIME

....
....
....
....
....

🕐 6A 7 8 9 10 11 12P 13 14 15 16 17 18 19 20 21 22+
B=BREAKFAST   L=LUNCH   D=DINNER   S=SNACKS   E=EXERCISE   M=MIND

HOW I FEEL

MO TU WE TH FR SA SU

DATE ....

DAY (66)

BREAKFAST

....
....
....
....
....

SNACKS

....
....
....
....

TOTAL CALORIES

_____

PROTEIN CONTENT FIBER CONTENT

_____ _____ _____

OTHER

....

LUNCH

....
....
....
....
....
....
....
....
....
....
....

DINNER

....
....
....
....
....

WEIGHT   SLEEP   WATER   PROTEIN

EXERCISE & ACTIVITY / MIND & SOUL   SET / REPS / DISTANCE   TIME

....
....
....
....
....

6A 7 8 9 10 11 12P 13 14 15 16 17 18 19 20 21 22+

B=BREAKFAST   L=LUNCH   D=DINNER   S=SNACKS   E=EXERCISE   M=MIND

DAY (67)

MO TU WE TH FR SA SU

DATE ....

BREAKFAST
....
....
....
....
....

SNACKS
....
....
....
....

LUNCH
....
....
....
....
....
....
....
....
....
....

DINNER
....
....
....
....
....
....
....
....
....
....

TOTAL CALORIES
_____ _____ _____

PROTEIN CONTENT   FIBER CONTENT

_____ _____ _____

WEIGHT	SLEEP	WATER	PROTEIN

OTHER
....

♥ EXERCISE & ACTIVITY / MIND & SOUL

	SET / REPS / DISTANCE	TIME
....	....	....
....	....	....
....	....	....
....	....	....
....	....	....

6A 7 8 9 10 11 12P 13 14 15 16 17 18 19 20 21 22+

B=BREAKFAST   L=LUNCH   D=DINNER   S=SNACKS   E=EXERCISE   M=MIND

HOW I FEEL

MO TU WE TH FR SA SU

DATE ....

DAY (68)

BREAKFAST

....
....
....
....
....
_____ ____ ____

SNACKS

....
....
....
....

LUNCH

....
....
....
....
....
....
....
....
....
....
____ ____ ____

DINNER

....
....
....
....
....
....
....
....
....
____ ____ ____

TOTAL CALORIES

_____ ____ ____

PROTEIN CONTENT   FIBER CONTENT

_____ ____ ____

WEIGHT · SLEEP · WATER · PROTEIN

==== ====   ....

OTHER

....

♥ EXERCISE & ACTIVITY / MIND & SOUL   SET / REPS / DISTANCE   TIME

....
....
....
....
....
_____ _____ _____

 6A 7 8 9 10 11 12P 13 14 15 16 17 18 19 20 21 22+

B=BREAKFAST   L=LUNCH   D=DINNER   S=SNACKS   E=EXERCISE   M=MIND

DAY (69)

MO TU WE TH FR SA SU

DATE ....

HOW I FEEL

BREAKFAST	LUNCH	DINNER
....	....	....
....	....	....
....	....	....
....	....	....
....	....	....

_____ ____
SNACKS

....
....
....
....

TOTAL CALORIES
_____

PROTEIN CONTENT FIBER CONTENT

| WEIGHT | SLEEP | WATER | PROTEIN |

____ ____

OTHER
....

 EXERCISE & ACTIVITY / MIND & SOUL   SET / REPS / DISTANCE   TIME

....	....	....
....	....	....
....	....	....
....	....	....
....	....	....

6A 7 8 9 10 11 12P 13 14 15 16 17 18 19 20 21 22+

B=BREAKFAST L=LUNCH D=DINNER S=SNACKS E=EXERCISE M=MIND

HOW I FEEL

😃 😊 😐 😞
○ ○ ○ ○

MO TU WE TH FR SA SU

DATE ....

DAY (70)

BREAKFAST

....
....
....
....
....

SNACKS

....
....
....
....

TOTAL CALORIES

_____ ___ ___

PROTEIN CONTENT FIBER CONTENT

_____ ___ ___

OTHER

....

LUNCH

....
....
....
....
....
....
....
....
....
....
....
....
....

DINNER

....
....
....
....
....
....
....
....
....
....
....
....
....

WEIGHT   **SLEEP**   **WATER**   **PROTEIN**

❤ **EXERCISE & ACTIVITY / MIND & SOUL**   SET / REPS / DISTANCE   TIME

....
....
....
....
....

 6A 7 8 9 10 11 12P 13 14 15 16 17 18 19 20 21 22+

B=BREAKFAST L=LUNCH D=DINNER S=SNACKS E=EXERCISE M=MIND

DAY (71)

MO TU WE TH FR SA SU

DATE ....

HOW I FEEL

BREAKFAST

LUNCH

DINNER

....
....
....
....
....

SNACKS

....
....
....
....

TOTAL CALORIES

_____

PROTEIN CONTENT FIBER CONTENT

_____   _____

OTHER

....

WEIGHT   SLEEP   WATER   PROTEIN

 EXERCISE & ACTIVITY / MIND & SOUL   SET / REPS / DISTANCE   TIME

6A 7   8   9   10   11   12P 13   14   15   16   17   18   19   20   21   22+

B=BREAKFAST   L=LUNCH   D=DINNER   S=SNACKS   E=EXERCISE   M=MIND

HOW I FEEL

MO TU WE TH FR SA SU

DATE ....

DAY (72)

BREAKFAST

....

....

....

....

....

_____ ____ ____

SNACKS

....

....

....

....

LUNCH

....

....

....

....

....

....

....

....

....

....

....

....

....

DINNER

....

....

....

....

....

....

....

....

....

....

TOTAL CALORIES

_____

PROTEIN CONTENT   FIBER CONTENT

_____ ____ ____

WEIGHT   SLEEP   WATER   PROTEIN

==================== ....

OTHER

....

EXERCISE & ACTIVITY / MIND & SOUL

SET / REPS / DISTANCE   TIME

....

....

....

....

....

6A 7 8 9 10 11 12P 13 14 15 16 17 18 19 20 21 22+

B=BREAKFAST L=LUNCH D=DINNER S=SNACKS E=EXERCISE M=MIND

DAY (73)

MO TU WE TH FR SA SU

DATE ....

HOW I FEEL

BREAKFAST	LUNCH	DINNER
....	....	....
....	....	....
....	....	....
....	....	....
....	....	....

SNACKS

....
....
....
....

TOTAL CALORIES
_____

PROTEIN CONTENT   FIBER CONTENT   WEIGHT   SLEEP   WATER   PROTEIN

OTHER
....

♥ EXERCISE & ACTIVITY / MIND & SOUL   SET / REPS / DISTANCE   TIME

.... | .... | ....
.... | .... | ....
.... | .... | ....
.... | .... | ....
.... | .... | ....

🕐 6A 7 8 9 10 11 12P 13 14 15 16 17 18 19 20 21 22+

B=BREAKFAST   L=LUNCH   D=DINNER   S=SNACKS   E=EXERCISE   M=MIND

HOW I FEEL

MO TU WE TH FR SA SU

DATE ....

DAY (74)

BREAKFAST	LUNCH	DINNER
....	....	....
....	....	....
....	....	....
....	....	....
....	....	....

SNACKS

TOTAL CALORIES

PROTEIN CONTENT   FIBER CONTENT   WEIGHT   SLEEP   WATER   PROTEIN

OTHER

♡ **EXERCISE & ACTIVITY / MIND & SOUL**   SET / REPS / DISTANCE   TIME

   6A   7   8   9   10   11   12P   13   14   15   16   17   18   19   20   21   22+

B=BREAKFAST   L=LUNCH   D=DINNER   S=SNACKS   E=EXERCISE   M=MIND

DAY (75)

DATE ....

HOW I FEEL

BREAKFAST

....
....
....
....
....
_____ ___ ___

SNACKS

....
....
....
....
_____ ___ ___

TOTAL CALORIES

_____

PROTEIN CONTENT   FIBER CONTENT

_____ ___

OTHER

....

LUNCH

....
....
....
....
....
....
....
....
....
....
....
....
....
....

DINNER

....
....
....
....
....
....
....
....
....
....
....
___ ___ ___

WEIGHT   SLEEP   WATER   PROTEIN

=========   ....

EXERCISE & ACTIVITY / MIND & SOUL

	SET / REPS / DISTANCE	TIME
....	....	....
....	....	....
....	....	....
....	....	....
....	....	....

 6A 7 8 9 10 11 12P 13 14 15 16 17 18 19 20 21 22+

B=BREAKFAST L=LUNCH D=DINNER S=SNACKS E=EXERCISE M=MIND

HOW I FEEL

MO TU WE TH FR SA SU

DATE ....

DAY (76)

BREAKFAST

....

....

....

....

....

_____ ___ ___

SNACKS

....

....

....

....

TOTAL CALORIES

_____

PROTEIN CONTENT   FIBER CONTENT

_____ ___ ___

OTHER

....

LUNCH

....

....

....

....

....

....

....

....

....

....

....

DINNER

....

....

....

....

....

....

....

....

....

WEIGHT

SLEEP

WATER

PROTEIN

_____ _____ ....

❤ EXERCISE & ACTIVITY / MIND & SOUL   SET / REPS / DISTANCE   TIME

....

....

....

....

....

6A 7 8 9 10 11 12P 13 14 15 16 17 18 19 20 21 22+

B=BREAKFAST   L=LUNCH   D=DINNER   S=SNACKS   E=EXERCISE   M=MIND

DAY (77)

MO TU WE TH FR SA SU

DATE ....

HOW I FEEL

BREAKFAST

....
....
....
....
....
_____ __ __

SNACKS

....
....
....
....
_____ __ __

TOTAL CALORIES

_____

PROTEIN CONTENT FIBER CONTENT

_____ _____

OTHER

....

LUNCH

....
....
....
....
....
....
....
....
....
....
....
....

DINNER

....
....
....
....
....

WEIGHT SLEEP WATER PROTEIN

_____ _____
_____ ....

❤〰 EXERCISE & ACTIVITY / MIND & SOUL   SET / REPS / DISTANCE   TIME

....
....
....
....
....
_____   _____   _____

🕐 6A 7 8 9 10 11 12P 13 14 15 16 17 18 19 20 21 22+
....
B=BREAKFAST   L=LUNCH   D=DINNER   S=SNACKS   E=EXERCISE   M=MIND

HOW I FEEL

😄 ☺ 😐 🙁
○ ○ ○ ○

MO TU WE TH FR SA SU

DATE ....

DAY (78)

BREAKFAST	LUNCH	DINNER
....	....	....
....	....	....
....	....	....
....	....	....
....	....	....

SNACKS

....	....	....
....	....	....
....	....	....
....	....	....

TOTAL CALORIES

_____

PROTEIN CONTENT FIBER CONTENT

WEIGHT   SLEEP   WATER   PROTEIN

OTHER
....

❤️ EXERCISE & ACTIVITY / MIND & SOUL   SET / REPS / DISTANCE   TIME

....	....	....
....	....	....
....	....	....
....	....	....
....	....	....

🕐 6A 7 8 9 10 11 12P 13 14 15 16 17 18 19 20 21 22+

B=BREAKFAST L=LUNCH D=DINNER S=SNACKS E=EXERCISE M=MIND

DAY (79)

MO TU WE TH FR SA SU

DATE ....

○ ○ ○ ○

BREAKFAST	LUNCH	DINNER
....	....	....
....	....	....
....	....	....
....	....	....
....	....	....

SNACKS

.... | .... | ....
.... | .... | ....
.... | .... | ....
.... | .... | ....

TOTAL CALORIES

_____

PROTEIN CONTENT   FIBER CONTENT   WEIGHT   SLEEP   WATER   PROTEIN

_____ _____   ========   ....

OTHER

....

♥ EXERCISE & ACTIVITY / MIND & SOUL   SET / REPS / DISTANCE   TIME

.... | .... | ....
.... | .... | ....
.... | .... | ....
.... | .... | ....
.... | .... | ....

🕐 6A 7 8 9 10 11 12P 13 14 15 16 17 18 19 20 21 22+

B=BREAKFAST   L=LUNCH   D=DINNER   S=SNACKS   E=EXERCISE   M=MIND

HOW I FEEL

MO TU WE TH FR SA SU

DATE ....

DAY (80)

BREAKFAST

....
....
....
....
....

_____ ____ ____

SNACKS

....
....
....
....

LUNCH

....
....
....
....
....
....
....
....
....
....
....
....
....

DINNER

....
....
....
....
....
....
....
....
....
....
....
....
....

TOTAL CALORIES

_____

PROTEIN CONTENT   FIBER CONTENT

_____ ____ ____

OTHER

....

WEIGHT   SLEEP   WATER   PROTEIN

=========== ==========   ....

♡ EXERCISE & ACTIVITY / MIND & SOUL   SET / REPS / DISTANCE   TIME

....
....
....
....
....

6A 7 8 9 10 11 12P 13 14 15 16 17 18 19 20 21 22+

B=BREAKFAST   L=LUNCH   D=DINNER   S=SNACKS   E=EXERCISE   M=MIND

DAY (81)

MO TU WE TH FR SA SU

DATE ....

BREAKFAST
....
....
....
....
....
—————————   ——————

SNACKS
....
....
....
....
————— —— ——————

TOTAL CALORIES
—————————————————————

PROTEIN CONTENT   FIBER CONTENT
—————————   ——————

LUNCH
....
....
....
....
....
....
....
....
....
....
....

DINNER
....
....
....
....
....
....
....
....
....

WEIGHT   SLEEP   WATER   PROTEIN

OTHER
....

♥ EXERCISE & ACTIVITY / MIND & SOUL   SET / REPS / DISTANCE   TIME
....
....
....
....
....

🕐 6A 7 8 9 10 11 12P 13 14 15 16 17 18 19 20 21 22+

B=BREAKFAST   L=LUNCH   D=DINNER   S=SNACKS   E=EXERCISE   M=MIND

HOW I FEEL

😃 ☺ 😐 ☹
○ ○ ○ ○

MO TU WE TH FR SA SU

DATE ....

DAY (82)

BREAKFAST

....

....

....

....

....

—————— ——— ———

SNACKS

....

....

....

....

LUNCH

....

....

....

....

....

....

....

....

....

....

....

....

DINNER

....

....

....

....

....

....

TOTAL CALORIES

—————— ——— ———

PROTEIN CONTENT   FIBER CONTENT

—————— ——— ———

OTHER

....

WEIGHT	SLEEP	WATER	PROTEIN

❤ EXERCISE & ACTIVITY / MIND & SOUL   SET / REPS / DISTANCE   TIME

....

....

....

....

....

 6A 7 8 9 10 11 12P 13 14 15 16 17 18 19 20 21 22+

B=BREAKFAST L=LUNCH D=DINNER S=SNACKS E=EXERCISE M=MIND

DAY (83)

MO TU WE TH FR SA SU

DATE ....

HOW I FEEL

BREAKFAST

....
....
....
....
....

——————— —— ———

SNACKS

....
....
....
....

LUNCH

....
....
....
....
....
....
....
....
....
....

DINNER

....
....
....
....

TOTAL CALORIES

———————————————

PROTEIN CONTENT   FIBER CONTENT

——————— —— ———

OTHER

....

WEIGHT   **SLEEP**   **WATER**   **PROTEIN**

....

♥ EXERCISE & ACTIVITY / MIND & SOUL

SET / REPS / DISTANCE   TIME

....
....
....
....
....

6A 7 8 9 10 11 12P 13 14 15 16 17 18 19 20 21 22+

B=BREAKFAST   L=LUNCH   D=DINNER   S=SNACKS   E=EXERCISE   M=MIND

HOW I FEEL

MO TU WE TH FR SA SU

DATE ....

DAY 84

BREAKFAST

....
....
....
....
....

SNACKS

....
....
....
....

LUNCH

....
....
....
....
....
....
....
....
....
....

DINNER

....
....
....
....
....
....
....
....
....

TOTAL CALORIES

PROTEIN CONTENT FIBER CONTENT

WEIGHT

SLEEP

WATER

PROTEIN

OTHER
....

EXERCISE & ACTIVITY / MIND & SOUL

SET / REPS / DISTANCE

TIME

....
....
....
....
....

6A 7 8 9 10 11 12P 13 14 15 16 17 18 19 20 21 22+

B=BREAKFAST L=LUNCH D=DINNER S=SNACKS E=EXERCISE M=MIND

DAY (85)

MO TU WE TH FR SA SU

DATE ....

BREAKFAST	LUNCH	DINNER
....	....	....
....	....	....
....	....	....
....	....	....
....	....	....

SNACKS

....

....

....

....

TOTAL CALORIES

_____

PROTEIN CONTENT   FIBER CONTENT

OTHER

....

....

WEIGHT   **SLEEP**   **WATER**   **PROTEIN**

♥ EXERCISE & ACTIVITY / MIND & SOUL   SET / REPS / DISTANCE   TIME

....	....	....
....	....	....
....	....	....
....	....	....
....	....	....

🕐 6A 7 8 9 10 11 12P 13 14 15 16 17 18 19 20 21 22+

B=BREAKFAST   L=LUNCH   D=DINNER   S=SNACKS   E=EXERCISE   M=MIND

HOW I FEEL

MO TU WE TH FR SA SU

DATE ....

DAY 86

BREAKFAST

....

....

....

....

....

____ ___ ___

SNACKS

....

....

....

....

....

LUNCH

....

....

....

....

....

....

....

....

....

....

....

....

____ ___ ___

DINNER

....

....

....

....

....

....

....

TOTAL CALORIES

_____

PROTEIN CONTENT   FIBER CONTENT

_____ _____ _____

OTHER

....

WEIGHT   **SLEEP**   **WATER**   **PROTEIN**

========
========   ....

♥ EXERCISE & ACTIVITY / MIND & SOUL   SET / REPS / DISTANCE   TIME

....

....

....

....

....

 6A 7 8 9 10 11 12P 13 14 15 16 17 18 19 20 21 22+

B=BREAKFAST L=LUNCH D=DINNER S=SNACKS E=EXERCISE M=MIND

DAY (87)

MO TU WE TH FR SA SU

DATE ....

BREAKFAST

....
....
....
....
....
———————— —— ——

SNACKS

....
....
....
....
———————— —— ——

LUNCH

....
....
....
....
....
....
....
....
....
....
....
....
....

DINNER

....
....
....
....
....
....
———————— —— ——

TOTAL CALORIES

————————————————

PROTEIN CONTENT FIBER CONTENT
———————— ————————

WEIGHT

SLEEP

WATER

PROTEIN

OTHER

....

❤ EXERCISE & ACTIVITY / MIND & SOUL   SET / REPS / DISTANCE   TIME

....
....
....
....
....
————————————

6A 7 8 9 10 11 12P 13 14 15 16 17 18 19 20 21 22+

B=BREAKFAST   L=LUNCH   D=DINNER   S=SNACKS   E=EXERCISE   M=MIND

HOW I FEEL

DAY (88)

MO TU WE TH FR SA SU

DATE ....

BREAKFAST	LUNCH	DINNER

SNACKS

TOTAL CALORIES

WEIGHT   SLEEP   WATER   PROTEIN

PROTEIN CONTENT   FIBER CONTENT

OTHER

♥ EXERCISE & ACTIVITY / MIND & SOUL   SET / REPS / DISTANCE   TIME

 6A   7   8   9   10   11   12P   13   14   15   16   17   18   19   20   21   22+

B=BREAKFAST   L=LUNCH   D=DINNER   S=SNACKS   E=EXERCISE   M=MIND

DAY (89)

MO TU WE TH FR SA SU

DATE ....

HOW I FEEL

BREAKFAST

LUNCH

DINNER

....
....
....
....
....
_____ ____ ____

SNACKS

....
....
....
....
_____ ____ ____

TOTAL CALORIES

_____

PROTEIN CONTENT FIBER CONTENT

_____ _____

WEIGHT

SLEEP

WATER

PROTEIN

OTHER

____ ____ _____ ════════ ....

....

♥ EXERCISE & ACTIVITY / MIND & SOUL

SET / REPS / DISTANCE

TIME

....
....
....
....
....
_____

🕐 6A 7 8 9 10 11 12P 13 14 15 16 17 18 19 20 21 22+
....
B=BREAKFAST L=LUNCH D=DINNER S=SNACKS E=EXERCISE M=MIND

HOW I FEEL

MO TU WE TH FR SA SU

DATE ....

DAY (90)

BREAKFAST	LUNCH	DINNER
....		....
....		....
....		....
....		....
....		....

SNACKS

....

....

....

....

TOTAL CALORIES

_____

PROTEIN CONTENT   FIBER CONTENT

WEIGHT   SLEEP   WATER   PROTEIN

OTHER

....

♡ **EXERCISE & ACTIVITY / MIND & SOUL**   SET / REPS / DISTANCE   TIME

....	....	....
....	....	....
....	....	....
....	....	....
....	....	....

🕐   6A 7 8 9 10 11 12P 13 14 15 16 17 18 19 20 21 22+

B=BREAKFAST   L=LUNCH   D=DINNER   S=SNACKS   E=EXERCISE   M=MIND

DAY 90

ARM ....

CHEST ....

WAIST ....

BELLY ....

HIP ....

THIGH ....

CALF ....

WEIGHT

BMI

....

NOTES ....
....
....
....
....

MY RESULTS

DAY **1**   DAY **90**   DIFFERENCE

ARM

CHEST

WAIST

BELLY

HIP

THIGH

CALF

WEIGHT   WEIGHT   WEIGHT

BMI   BMI   BMI

NOTES

COPYRIGHT © CUTE FOOD DIARY IDEAS
PUBLISHED BY: STUDIO 5519, 1732 1ST AVE #25519 NEW YORK, NY 10128
APRIL 2017, ISSUE NO. 1 [V 1.0]: CONTACT: INFO@STUDIO5519.COM: ILLUSTRATION CREDITS: © DEPOSITPHOTOS / @ PUSH☰KA11 / @ GLEB_GURALNYK

CPSIA information can be obtained
at www.ICGtesting.com
Printed in the USA
FSHW02n2128140618
49442FS